Lionel Knight
65 Badshot Park
Badshot Lea
Farnham
Surrey
GU9 9NE

C000242803

"A rather sad beginning ...

S/L P A Gilchrist DFC

The Story of Halifax L9489

researched and written by Dennis Hoppe

I dedicate my researches and this booklet to my wife, Valerie, and to our sons, Paul and David who, at 27 and 24,are the same age as so many aircrew who never returned from operations. May our children and their generation never be called upon to make the same sacrifice for the sake of freedom and peace in the world.

Farnham January 1998

Published by VaaVee Books
Farnham GU10 4SZ   01252 793010

ISBN 0 9532914 0 5

Printed by the Phoenix Press Ltd
Units 12-14 Enterprise Estate
Station Road West
Ash Vale Surrey GU15 5QJ
Tel: 01252 547799 Fax: 01252 543355

Writer's Note

A memorable part of my boyhood was spent gazing up in wonderment at the air battles raging overhead in the cloudless azure skies. It was the summer of 1940. Like my contemporaries, I longed to be up there too. Was it little wonder that those stirring events should not have aroused in me, and many of my generation, an interest in aviation which has endured through the years.

Worthing, close to the RAF airfields at Tangmere, Westhampnett, Ford and Shoreham, was, during those perilous days, in the front-line of a dire struggle for our country's freedom. The civilian population, old and young, was very much part of this conflict. Casualties there were, and often high, but amid the sadness there was a spirit of unity and tenacity of purpose throughout the kingdom that was to last for another five long and demanding years.

And so, in retirement fifty-five years later, and living in Aldershot, I turned to my lifelong interest to which now I could devote more time.

Whilst scanning the pages of "Bomber Command Losses" (Vol 2) by W R Chorley, a single, stark statistic came to light: a Halifax bomber of 35 Squadron had crashed in nearby Normandy; the year: 1941.

This was the first operational sortie flown by the new four-engined aircraft and, mistakenly, it had been shot down by one of our own night fighters. Four airman had died; two had survived.

Behind such tragedies there lies a story of courage and fortitude.

An initial visit to the graveyard of the parish church of St Mark, Wyke, Normandy, and a chance conversation with an elderly inhabitant, yielded little information. It was a letter to the Surrey Advertiser, in November 1994, that brought an encouraging response which led to contacts with Bob Wye, Peter Harms and Beryl Chandler. All three had been children in 1941 and remembered the night the aircraft had crashed into a field close to their homes.

With their assistance the site was located and later verified by Colin Pratley of the Croydon Aviation Archaeological Society.

And thus an intriguing story was about to unfold.

Introduction**Sunday 9 March 1997**

I am a 78-year-old ancient aviator standing in Minty's field in the grounds of Merrist Wood Agricultural College, Worplesdon, Surrey, at the spot where Halifax L9489, 'F-Freddie', was shot down by "friendly fire" whilst returning from its first operational sortie on the night of 10 March 1941.

I believe I am the sole survivor of this first Halifax raid carried out by the newly re-formed 35 Squadron.

I am very privileged to be one of so many people remembering with gratitude those who died here - all comrades of mine - and to share in their proud sorrow.

These were brave young men, proud to be members of the Royal Air Force, committed to taking the initiative against the enemy in the early dark days of the war when the United Kingdom stood, virtually alone.

A good number of their surviving relatives are present today, remembering all that these young men meant, and continue to mean, to them. Fifty-six years have passed but the memories are fresh.

We listen to the Dedication, the prayers and the Last Post, and all around us is a "presence" that cannot be defined. Minty's field will always be a hallowed resting place.

Stanley Desmond Greaves DFM RAFVR
formerly Warrant Officer, Pilot, 35 Squadron, Linton-on-Ouse
Service No 754271

Stan Greaves photographed on the day of the dedication of our Memorial plaque 9 March 1997.
The sole living survivor of the first Halifax operation to Le Havre 10 March 1941. This remarkable veteran still enjoys flying.

The Crew
The Aircraft
The Squadron
The Base
The Operation
Eye Witness Accounts

S/L Peter 'Alex' Gilchrist DFC 37348
Captain

Peter Alexander Gilchrist was a Canadian born in Weyburn, Saskatchewan, in August 1910.
He gained his Private Pilot's Licence when he was 22 and because the rapidly developing RAF offered him the chance to fly, he enlisted in 1935 for a short-term 3-year commission.
Known to most as Peter, he was called Alec or Gil or Gillie in the Air Force.
Peter served overseas and flew Vickers Valentias in Iraq in 1937, with 70 Squadron, and returned to the United Kingdom later in the year to join 51 Squadron and its Whitley bombers.
During the early months of the war he took part in many 'Nickel' sorties, dropping leaflets on Berlin on one occasion. For his tenacity and flying skills his award of the DFC was promulgated on 1 June 1940. (He was to be Mentioned in Dispatches later in the war, in June 1942.)
Chosen to be among the first experienced and decorated pilots to fly the new Halifax heavy bomber, Peter Gilchrist joined the re-formed 35 Squadron at Boscombe Down in October 1940. There he flew the prototype, L7244 and was to say later, *"... the Halifax handled so well that I would land it hands off the control column by using the fore and aft trim wheel only - for the benefit of new pilots."*
After the traumatic first sortie when he had to abandon L9489, he wasloaned by the RAF to command the first Canadian heavy bomber squadron, number 405, initially at Driffield and then at Pocklington. As Wing Commander he led his pilots to attack the German pocket battleships, Scharnhorst and Gneisenau and the cruiser Prinz Eugen holed up in Brest. His Wellington, W5551, was shot down by a German fighter. This was 24 July 1941.

1

He and another crew member, who had also parachuted to safety, evaded capture and eventually returned to England, early in 1942, via Switzerland and Gibralter.

For security reasons, he was not permitted, as a senior officer who had avoided captivity, to fly over Europe again and was transferred to Coastal Command. There he commanded 120 and 59 Squadrons flying patrols over the Atlantic.

In February 1945 he applied, successfully, to join the RCAF and was promoted to Group Captain.

After the war, he remained in the Canadian Air Force and attained senior posts and pursued a distinguished career both at home and abroad. His love for flying remained and his postings enabled him to fly jet aircraft such as the F86 and the CF100.

In retirement, Peter enjoyed golf, shooting and skiing and was an active member of the Canadian branch of the RAF Escaping Society.

Air Commodore Peter Alexander Gilchrist died, after a brief illness, in Toronto on September 2 1990 leaving his wife, Ina, daughter, Carol, and grandchildren, David, Robert and Julia.

S/L Gilchrist: Log Book for March 1941 *(Photograph and Log Book by courtesy of the Henderson family)*

Sgt Reg Lucas
Pilot

741992

Reginald Lucas was born in Mansfield on 10 August 1911, the first of six children, two of whom survive today. From an early age he was brought up by his grandparents who doted upon him.
His father, Reg Lucas, Senior, started a motorcycle business and regularly took part in the Isle of Man TT Races and when Reg left Brunt's school at sixteen he entered the family business. Whilst still a teenager he rode for Nottingham Speedway team with some success and it was there that a fellow rider influenced him to join the RAF Volunteer Reserve. He then took to flying and gliding, and these became his chief hobbies.
From motorbikes he graduated to fast cars and having acquired a Bentley he was soon in trouble with the law being fined two guineas for driving, *"to the danger of the public at Kirkby."* There was laughter in the courtroom when Reg admitted that he had got *"the breeze up"* when he saw the policeman, stopped, and backed onto the footpath. (After the tragic crash of L9489, his father could not bear to be reminded of his son's youthful exuberance and promise, and he sold the car immediately for a mere pittance.)
Reg had gained his pilot's licence at Tollerton in 1935 and when war came he was among the first to be called-up.
Devotion to his Bentley was to land him in further trouble whilst he was serving with 19 OTU in October 1940. He came by some petrol through other than official channels and temporarily lost his rank as a result. (His sister, Nance, recalled that when her brother came home on leave at this time he borrowed another Sergeant's uniform top. By this subterfuge Reg hoped that his parents would not come to hear of his misdemeanour!)

3

Reg regained his Sergeant's stripes in January 1941 prior to his posting to 77 Squadron. For several weeks he took part in operations on Whitleys, and without mishap. It was on 24 February that he was transferred from Topcliffe to 35 Squadron at Linton-on-Ouse to serve as second pilot on the new Halifax bomber in the crew skippered by S/L Peter Gilchrist.

He was critically injured in the crash of "F-Freddie" and died in Guildford hospital the next day, having previously been reported as "missing".

Reg Lucas rests now in the Nottingham Road cemetery, Mansfield.

Reg Lucas Jnr: Nottingham Speedway circa 1930
(Lucas family)

Sergeant Ron Aedy
Flight Engineer

568825

Ronald Godfrey Aedy was born in Kingston upon Thames, Surrey, on 10 June1919.

His family emigrated to Canada and, as a boy, Ron helped his father on the farm in the wilds of Saskatchewen some sixty miles from Regina. No doubt, the vast open spaces and the expansive skies above nurtured a yearning to reach for the heavens, like so many other young men of his generation who had read of, and often seen, the daring exploits of the early aviators.

With flying on his mind he returned to England and was accepted for a twelve-year term of service in the Royal air Force. Thus began his apprenticeship at RAF Halton in 1936. He had become a 'Trenchard Brat'.

Although he retained his British nationality, he was proud of his years in the Dominion and his entitlement to wear the Canada flash on his uniform sleeve, which he did throughout the war years. Prior to his posting to 35 Squadron in November 1940, he had served with 29 and 242 Squadrons equipped with Blenheims and Hurricanes respectively. It was whilst he was servicing the latter single-engined fighters that he became familiar with the Rolls Royce Merlin engine which was to power the Halifax.

The 35 squadron ORB states, *"... 568825 Cpl Aedy R. G. (Fitter 2) promoted to rank of Sergeant w.e.f. 1.2.41 ... ... necessary for an engineer to be included in the aircrew to fly Halifax aircraft."* His previous experience with 242 Squadron was to stand him in good stead as a Flight Engineer on the new heavy bomber.

Just after 10 o'clock on that fatal night of 10 March 1941, Ron Aedy was the only crew member to be injured in the devastating attack

5

made by the British night fighter. He was seriously wounded in the leg and, on the orders of the Skipper, Squadron Leader Gilchrist, he was to be the first to leave the blazing aircraft, assisted by his friends. It was Sergeant Stan Broadhurst, the Wireless Operator who courageously held onto the ripcord as Ron was bundled out of the rear fuselage door. This was a selfless act of heroism that Ron Aedy was never to forget. His widow, Audrey, wrote of the affection and gratitude with which her husband always spoke of Stan Broadhurst. Maybe that was the underlying reason why he found it so difficult to forgive his fellow countryman who had brought about these four untimely and violent deaths, and caused Ron himself the physical injury which effectively ended his operational flying career.

In his report to Irvin, the parachute manufacturers, S/L Gilchrist reported that Sgt Aedy had lost consciousness after he left the aircraft. His landing was impeded by a tree and it was his cries in the night air that brought rescue and despatch to Guildford Hospital. He was later transferred to EMS Haywards Heath, where he was visited by his youthful cousin, Guy Jennings, who cycled all the way from Surbiton to see him. (Such was the precarious state of public transport at that time.)

Before he ended his service days, with the rank of Squadron Leader, Ron Aedy took every opportunity to fly as a passenger or an observer. He gained his glider pilot's licence in 1956, although his first solo flight almost ended in tragedy: the tow-rope broke quite suddenly and it took considerable skill before Ron was able to gain sufficient air speed to make a safe landing. Also, some years later, he was on board an RAF helicopter which crashed into the sea. Quick thinking enabled him and the crew to escape. Such was the man that some years after this incident, he undertook an ejection-seat test, *"just for the fun of it."*

He had overcome his physical injury by sheer determination, the limp which he inherited as a result of his wounds never prevented him from living life to the full.

6

As a family man, Ron had three children by his marriage to Alfreda, who had nursed him during his lengthy convalescence. (All are now living, with their families, in England.) Five more children were borne by his second wife, Audrey, one of whom works for the BBC in this country. Of his twelve grandchildren he lived to enjoy the company of only four.

Audrey Aedy wrote of her late husband, *"He was the total optimist and he was a merry-hearted man able to lift any occasion from something very ordinary to something very special by his enthusiasm and the force of his personality."*

And later, "What great loss, pain and despair that plane crash must have caused to so many families. What a futile business war is!"

Squadron Leader Ronald Godfrey Aedy died in Australia on 2 August 1985, aged 66.

Motorcycle Permit: S/L RG Aedy: RAF Kabrit, Egypt 1947
(Audrey Aedy)

7

P/O Teddy Arnold 77908
Observer

Edward Rolfe Arnold was born in Saham Toney, near Watton, in Norfolk, on 7 August 1915. His parents moved to Leatherhead, Surrey, five years later, where they soon became well known in the local business and church circles. Teddy sang in the choir and was an active member, with his father, of Toc H.
His early education began in the old CE Primary School and from there he moved on to Sutton County
School after passing the scholarship at eleven. From here he gained a place at King's College, London, and was selected to play both hockey and cricket whilst he was there.
As a member of German Jewish Aid he travelled yearly to Berlin and had many friends in Germany. His sister, Mrs Mary Millsted, recalls that her family had a close affinity with the German people through these links and that it grieved Teddy, especially, that he had to be prepared to drop bombs on his former friends.
He was fascinated by the exploits of Sir Alan Cobham and due to this interest in flying he joined the RAFVR in March 1939.
With the outbreak of war, he was called-up and trained in Canada and Bermuda before joining 35 Squadron as an Observer on the new Halifax bomber.
After his untimely death, Teddy's parents specifically requested that he be buried next to a German airman, Unteroffizier Wilhelm Mennigmann, who had been shot down over Dorking during the Battle of Britain. The two airmen, friend and foe, lay at peace side by side until Wilhelm was re-interred in his homeland after the war. Mrs Arnold tended both graves during those years and, when she was laid to rest, the wooden cross, which hung in the parish church where her son had been a sidesman, was placed in her coffin.

Pilot Officer Teddy Arnold's grave is to be found in the cemetery of the church where he and his family had worshipped, St Mary and St Nicholas with All Saints, Leatherhead.

George Dench, a remarkable ninety-two-year-old, and a lifelong family friend, has placed a solitary poppy on the grave each Armistice Day.

P/O Teddy Arnold. Somewhere in England 1940.
(Mary Millsted)

Sgt Stan Broadhurst

550817

Wireless Operator/Air Gunner

Stanley Broadhurst was born in 1920, one of eleven children. Unfortunately, his mother died when he was still young and his father could not cope with such a large family. Consequently, Stan and his brothers and sisters were fostered by family members and friends.

He was educated, as a boarder, at King Edward's School, Witley, in Surrey. (A boyhood friend remembered the young Stan coming home for his holidays in his sailor-boy suit - the official school uniform of the day.

From school he joined the RAF as a boy apprentice.

Little is known about his subsequent service career but, prior to his transfer to 35 Squadron, he served on 10 Squadron flying Whitleys. He was in the aircraft of his C/O, Wing Commander W E Staton, on the night of 1/2 October 1939, the first intrusion over Berlin - to drop nothing more lethal than leaflets - when, *"at 25,000 feet, the oxygen supply failed momentarily and Leading Aricraftsman Stan Broadhurst ... collapsed. Pilot Officer 'Lofty' Willis ... dragged Stan Broadhurst back to the cockpit and connected his tube to the main supply."**

His same friend, mentioned above, George Mallattrat, recalled that Stan was looking forward to his next leave as he was about to plan his 21st Birthday celebrations. Fate intervened and Stan Broadhurst never lived to see that day.

It is known that during the confusion provoked by the unexpected night fighter attack over Sussex and Surrey, he helped Peter Gilchrist to strap on his chest parachute, and he was the one to hold onto Ron

---

*"The Whitley Boys" by G L 'Larry' Donnelly p47 *(Air Research Publications 1991)*

10

Aedy's ripcord as the wounded and semi-conscious Flight Engineer was bundled out of the doomed aircraft. Like his friends who died with him, he thought of others well-being first.

He was laid to rest in Woodhouse Cemetery, Mansfield, the home town he shared with his pilot, Reg Lucas. (Poignantly and unusually, no next-of-kin details are recorded in the official register of the War Graves Commission.)

King Edward's School, Witley, Surrey, July 1867
(with permission)

F/O Bert Cooper

77963

Rear Gunner

Albert Edward Cooper was born in West Ham on 26 November 1906. He joined the Royal Navy when he was 21 and served for ten years until his discharge. Bert then worked as a window-frame fitter for Crittalls in Braintree, Essex, but volunteered for aircrew in 1940 and was granted a commission: Flying Officer.

He attended a course for Air Gunners at Warmwell and upon appointment to 35 Squadron he was made Gunnery Officer.

When he was killed he was 34 years of age and considered rather old for aircrew duties.

His mother, Mrs Hollock, had remarried after the death of his father and lived in Coggeshall, Essex. Her one regret was that she was not allowed to see her son prior to his burial as the undertakers had instructed that the coffin was not to be opened. (Maybe it was a blessing that she should remember him as he was and not live with the image of a son badly mutilated as a result of the crash in which he died.)

It would appear that Bert Cooper was either divorced or separated from his wife, Daisy, whom he had married in 1927, and had two children, Kenneth and Josephine. (Their present whereabouts is not known.)

A neighbour of Mrs Hollock said that as a young girl she remembers the coffin being removed from the house next door, *"covered with a huge cross of red roses, from a lady friend who I believe lived in London."*

Bert's mother had lost three sons in the Great War and was no stranger to death. (It is interesting that the newspaper report of the time, The Essex Weekly News, 21 March 1941, ascribes F/O Albert Cooper's death, *"as a result of enemy action."*)

The 'Last Post' and 'Reveille' were sounded by buglers of the Tank Corps at his commital.

The grave of F/O Bert Cooper: Coggeshall cemetery, Essex.
(Derrick & Janet Gray)

It was not possible to trace Flying Officer Cooper's children but his nephew, Paul Cooper, was present at the Dedication and provided details of his uncle's life and the service photograph.

.

The Aircraft: Halifax Mk I L9489

In response to the Air Ministry specification P.13/36, issued in August 1936, calling for a twin engined medium-heavy bomber, Handley Page designed HP56 and submitted a tender in March of the following year. However, the Rolls-Royce Vulture engines were not yet readily available and the specification was amended in September 1937 to incorporate a new design, HP57, with four Rolls-Royce Merlins which offered improved take-off power and proven reliability. Consequently, a contract was placed in January 1938 for the two prototypes already ordered and one hundred production Halifax Mk I machines, the first fifty being L9485-L9534. The new bomber entered service, with the re-formed 35 Squadron, at Boscombe Down in November 1940. Wg Cdr R W P Collings was the first CO. The squadron then moved to Leeming and finally to Linton-on-Ouse in December of the same year. It became operational in March 1941, with No 4 Bomber Group, a year before its more famous counterpart, the Lancaster, but a month after the Stirling's first sortie.

Our aircraft, L9489, the fifth production model, was built at Cricklewood, in the Handley Page factory, and flown from Radlett to be allocated to 37 MU where it was taken on charge on the 20 October 1940. It reached Linton-on-Ouse on 12 January 1941, ferried from Boscombe Down by F/L T P A Bradley and crew, to raise the squadron strength of Halifaxes to four. (Unfortunately, this was reduced to three when L9487, with F/O M T G Henry at the controls, crashed in flames on 13 January whilst on a test flight. There were no survivors.)

More aircraft arrived and an intensive training programme was embarked upon. By early March it was decided to introduce the new heavy bomber to operations. Le Havre was the target selected in line with a new policy.

Winston Churchill was preoccupied with the threat of the German U-

14

boat to the country's lifeline - supplies from abroad, chiefly the American continent, by way of Atlantic convoys. Hence Bomber Command was instructed to concentrate its efforts upon the destruction of submarine construction yards in Germany and operational bases along the French coast. For this reason, Le Havre, with its docks and submarine facilities, was the target selected for 35 Squadron's first operational flight with the new Halifax.

The total flying hours for L9489 is not stated on the AM Form 78, but the extent of damage is categorized: FBO (E) (Total Wreck). Thus ended her short life.

(It is sad to note that although a total of 6,176 Halifaxes were produced, only two complete airframes exist in the world today: at the RAF Museum, Hendon, and the Yorkshire Air Museum, Elvington, York.)

"Friday 13th" photographed at Elvington in 1996.*
(with permission YAM)

---

*In 1984 the derelict fuselage of Halifax HR792 was discovered in the Outer Hebrides, on the Isle of Lewis, in use as a hen coop! From this small beginning and thanks to the dedication and persistence of Ian Robinson and his team from the Yorkshire Air Museum at Elvington, Yorks, a Halifax was restored. Named after "Friday 13th", LV907 of 158 Squadron, she now stands proudly as a lasting memorial to the men and women who built, maintained and flew this most illustrious aircraft.

35 Squadron

1916-1982

'Madras Presidency'

35 Squadron was formed at Thetford in 1916 as a reconnaissance unit and moved to France in 1917, after initial training, and equipped with KF8s. It operated for the remainder of the war as an artillery support and photographic squadron co-operating closely with the cavalry. At the end of hostilities 35 Squadron returned to the UK and disbanded on 26 June 1919.

After a lapse of ten years, No 35 re-formed at Bircham Newton in March 1929 as a day bomber squadron with DH9As.

As a result of the Abyssinian crisis, the squadron moved to the Sudan in 1935 with its Fairey Gordons. The next year it was back in England and re-equipped with Wellesleys, to be followed by Battles in 1938.

During the early months of the war it became a training unit with a variety of aircraft, and then combined with 207 Squadron to become No 17 Operational training Unit. This was on 8 April 1940.

On 5 November 1940, 35 re-formed once again, this time to introduce the second four-engined heavy bomber to enter service with the RAF: the Halifax. Its first, and ill-fated operation was flown on the night of 10 March 1941 to Le Havre. Of the six aircraft dispatched, 'F-Freddie' was destined not to return to base at Linton-on-Ouse.

In 1942 the squadron was transferred to the Pathfinder Force and in 1944 converted to Lancasters for the remainder of the war.

A goodwill tour to America took place in 1946 and, after re-equipping with Lincolns three years later, 35 was disbanded in 1950. However, the squadron was to be re-formed when Washingtons began to arrive from America as a stop-gap measure prior to the arrival on the new jet bombers. This was at Marham. Subsequently, Canberras arrived in 1954 and were based in Cyprus during the Suez crisis.

Once more the squadron was disbanded, at Upwood: 1961.

True to form, it was only a short time before 35 became a service unit again. This time, in 1962, at Coningsby when Vulcan B2s were its new aircraft. For six years the squadron was abroad, stationed in Akrotiri.

Inevitably, 35 was disbanded for the last time, it would seem, on 28 February 1982.

Thus, another glorious chapter in the history of the RAF had been finally written. Many great names will be recalled and the roll of honour remain lengthy, but the memory of one particular aircraft will always be inscribed in 35 Squadron's battle honours: Halifax L9489, 'F-Freddie':

took part in first operation flown by Halifaxes; target Le Havre; mission completed; shot down over the home counties by a British night fighter; four crew died, two survived, one seriously injured.

"Uno Animo Agimus"

Viewing area 1996

Opened in May 1937, RAF Linton-on-Ouse was part of the expansion programme airfields. It boasted no less than five large C type hangars and the buildings were of a high specification.

It became the headquarters station of No 4 Group and numbers 51 and 58 Squadrons took up residence with their Whitley bombers, to be joined later by 77, 78 and 102 Squadrons.

At the end of 1940 the first Halifax of the re-formed 35 Squadron arrived. (L9489 was ferried in by F/L TPA Bradley,DFC, on 12 January 1941.)

In 1943 the airfield was handed over to No 6 Group, RCAF, when 77 and 78 Squadrons moved out. Their places were taken by the Lancaster Mk 11s of 426 and, later, 408. Both squadrons remained at Linton until the end of the war having re-equipped with Halifaxes during 1944.

From June 1945 the airfield was returned to the RAF and No 1665 Conversion Unit of Transport Command took over.

For the first time in its life, Linton became a fighter base in 1946 when Mosquitoes (246), Hornets (64 and 65) and, later, Meteors, Sabres and Hunters (66 and 92) took up residence.

However, 246 Squadron flew out with its Hunters in 1957 and the airfield was to re-open later in the year as a Flying Training Command station. Today the airfield is active as No1 FTS equipped with Tucanos for basic and advanced training.

The Jet Provost gate guardian serves as a reminder of the station's longstanding role in the training of future pilots for the RAF and RN.

In contrast, the Memorial Room, founded by Bill Steel and now in the caring hands of Peter Naylor, is a tribute to the men and women who were stationed at Linton when Whitleys, Halifaxes and Lancasters thundered off to war during those fateful years 1939 to 1945.

For further reading Peter Mason's 'Wings over Linton' is highly recommended.

The Operation   Le Havre: 10 March 1941

Seven Halifax Mk1s were prepared for this the inaugural operation to be flown by the second heavyweight bomber to be introduced into Bomber Command in 1941. (The Short Stirling had beaten its counterpart by one month when, on February 10, three of these aircraft from 7 Squadron were part of a mixed force which attacked Rotterdam.)

A message was received at Linton-on-Ouse from the Air Officer Commanding, Air marshal Sir Richard Peirse, addressed to the Commanding Officer of 35 Squadron: *"Good wishes to 35 Squadron and the heavyweights on the opening of their Halifax operations tonight. I hope the full weight of the Squadron's blows will soon be felt further afield."*

Seven aircraft were readied by ground crews during the day but, in the event, only six proved to be serviceable, the seventh suffering hydraulic failure.

In perfect weather the first Halifax, L9486, piloted by Wing Commander Collings, took off at 19.00 hours. Squadron Leader Gilchrist was the third to leave the ground at 19.08 hours. He successfully located the target and bombed from 11,800 feet but, unfortunately, due to thickening cloud, results were not observed.

Four of the force were able to bomb the primary target; one other attacked Dieppe, the secondary target, whilst the sixth aircraft jettisoned its bombs in the Channel. Flying Officer Warren, in L9493, was hit by flack and 'G-George' was damaged. *(cf reports by Stan Greaves and 'Oggie' Ogden which follow.)*

It was whilst these Halifaxes were heading for home over the United Kingdom that our aircraft, L9489, was unexpectedly fired upon by a British night fighter. The starboard outer engine caught fire and this spread rapidly to the inner engine engulfing the wing in flames. Sergeant Lucas was at the controls when 'F-Freddie' was hit and

Sergeant Aedy, the flight engineer, severely wounded by shrapnel. Peter Gilchrist, who had been enjoying a flask of coffee at once took command and ordered his wounded crew member to be assisted with his parachute. He was to be the first to leave.

The order to abandon the aircraft was given but, it would appear that this instruction was not heard by the crew owing to the intercomm having been shot away. Also, the front escape hatch had jammed in the initial confusion. The Skipper left the stricken bomber through the escape exit above the pilot's seat and was badly bruised when he struck one of the tail fins.

In bundling the injured airman out of the main fuselage door and ensuring that his ripcord was pulled as he left, it is probable that there was no time for the remaining four crew to parachute to safety themselves. They had sacrificed their own lives to save that of their friend. *(Cf the chapter devoted to Ron Aedy, and the scriptural text chosen for the memorial plaque.)*

The aircraft had been seen, *"falling like a flaming torch from the sky"* as one eyewitness put it. It hit the ground in a corner of Minty's field, Normandy, near Aldershot, at 10.40 hours on that fatal night of 10 march 1941. Rescue services were soon on the spot but there was little they could do for the four crew who had not been able to escape from the doomed aircraft. The surface wreckage was guarded by the local Home Guard until it was removed soon afterwards. The port inner engine and much of the forward section of L9489 remained in the ground until unearthed fifty-five years later.

Of the two survivors, Peter Gilchrist landed in a field of cattle, opposite the Duke of Normandy public house and about a quarter of a mile from the crash site. Ron Aedy lost consciousness during his descent, owing to his loss of blood, and had to be rescued from trees which had snagged his parachute. His cries brought help and he was soon in hospital in Guildford.

And thus the first, and last, operational mission of 'F-Freddie' had ended in disaster and unnecessary loss of human life.

Today this quiet corner of a Surrey field remains a shrine to the memory of those young men who, typical of their generation, gave their lives in the cause of freedom and peace.

Minty's Field, Merrist Wood: prior to landscaping

Full Circle
An Airman's Story 1

"I am a twenty-one-year-old Sergeant Pilot flying Whitley bombers with No 58 Squadron based at Royal Air Force Station, Linton-on-Ouse, Yorkshire. I have now completed five operational sorties as a Second Pilot and will shortly be in command of my own aircraft and crew.

A few days ago the Halifax prototype (in training livery) overflew Linton bound for Leeming where, it is rumoured, No 35 Squadron is being re-formed.

I remember sighing, wistfully, at the sight of this superb four-engined bomber, still on the secret list, and wondering if ever I would be privileged to fly it.

It is now mid-December and the Halifax has been transferred to Linton! 35 Squadron will be re-formed here instead of Leeming. Six operational aircraft are expected in the near future and training will commence without delay.

I cannot believe my good fortune. I am posted to 35 Squadron to convert on to the Halifax!

Monday, 10 March, 1941
All preliminary flight testing and crew training has been completed and the first six Halifax Mk1 aircraft are ready for battle. Tonight is to be our baptism of fire!

We have been briefed to attack the docks and shipping at the French port of Le Havre from a height of 12,000'. 'G-George' will be our aircraft and was flight-tested this afternoon. Take off will be at one minute intervals and each aircraft will operate individually. Strict radio silence is to be observed.

Now it is late evening. There is anticipation and excitement, and we are 'raring to go'.

Twenty-four mighty Merlins burst into life and we slowly taxi towards the holding point in line astern. The green light flashes, the four throttles are pushed fully open and we speed along the runway climbing away and setting our course. The night sky is clear and visibility is good. The journey south is uneventful, but as 'G-George' nears the French coast the weather is deteriorating; thickening cloud is building, and at 12,000' it is difficult to locate the docks area. We circle and, when the target clears, we drop our bombs and see the flashes as they explode. Almost immediately we are hit by shrapnel; the starboard inner engine is badly damaged and losing coolant. The engine has to be 'feathered' to prevent overheating, and the starboard undercarriage leg drops down as the hydraulics are affected. The enemy anti-aircraft fire is surprisingly accurate. Sgt Wilson, our observer and bomb-aimer, lying in a prone position in the nose of the aircraft, has been wounded in the right leg. He is helped back to the rest couch; a morphine injection is administered and a 'shell-dressing' is applied. We turn onto a northerly heading and, as we cross the south coast of England, the visibility improves. 'G-George' growls along on three engines and we soon see Linton's red beacon at a distance of more than forty miles. During our flight we have not sighted another aircraft, either friend or foe! It occurs to me that we may be the first Halifax to be damaged by enemy action. We make a safe landing and an ambulance takes Sgt. Wilson to York hospital for an immediate operation.

At de-briefing we learn that, as yet, nothing has been heard from 'F-Freddie' flown by our Flight Commander, Squadron Leader P A Gilchrist.

After a light meal and a short sleep I drive to York on my motor-bike and I am with Sgt Wilson when he comes out of the anaesthetic. Apparently, his right knee-cap has been removed, but otherwise he seems all right

I shall not be needed tonight, so I drive to my home in Bradford, where my parents live, and snatch a little more sleep before riding back to Linton on Wednesday morning ready for operations to

Hamburg.

I hear the tragic news that 'F-Freddie' has been shot down by one of our own night fighters - at a place called Normandy, near Aldershot. Four airmen, comrades of mine, are dead. Squadron Leader Gilchrist and his Flight Engineer, Sgt Aedy, have survived.

The first Halifax sortie of the 1939-45 war has been very much a 'baptism of fire'."

Sergeant Stan Greaves

Target: Le Havre 10 March 1941
An Airman's Story 2

"I joined the Royal Air Force as an Aircraft Fitter in January, 1936. I passed out as a Fitter 2 and joined 40 Bomber Squadron in January 1939 and served with them on Fairey Battles. We proceeded to France on 2nd September 1939 but returned to England in December to re-equip with Blenheims and later Wellingtons.

In November 1940 I was posted to the Halifax Development Unit at RAF Boscombe Down. The day I arrived, the unit was re-designated 35 Squadron and posted to RAF Leeming, in Yorkshire. A few weeks later the Squadron moved to RAF Linton-on-Ouse.

The CO of 35 Squadron was Wing Commander Collings, who had been awarded the AFC, and his Flight Engineer, Sergeant Watts, the AFM, for their work in developing the Halifax aircraft.

All the NCO Fitters on the squadron were invited by the CO to volunteer for duties as Flight Engineers. Apart from Sergeant Watts, who had already volunteered, Corporals Aedy, Ploughman, Wheeler and myself (all ex Halton Apprentices) volunteered, and after intensive training on the squadron and considerable flying training development, were promoted to Sergeants.

Sergeant Ploughman was killed in a flying accident shortly before the Squadron's first operation.*

I was teamed up with Flying Officer Warren DFC and we were allotted L9493.

The first Halifax operation took place on the night of 10th March 1941. This operation was described as a Nursery Operation and was to be an attack on German barge concentrations, dock installations and military targets at Le Havre, France.

I was flying as Flight Engineer in Halifax L9493. The Captain was

---

*This was the loss of L9487. On test this aircraft was seen at 8, 000' with the undercarriage down and trailing flames and smoke. It crashed 4 miles north of Dishforth on 13 January 1941.

Flying Officer Warren DFC who had considerable operational experience on Whitleys. All the crews, with the exceptions of the Flight Engineers, had completed a full tour on No 4 Group squadrons. They gave me vivid descriptions of what to expect and told me not to worry about lights flashing past or bangs on the wings or fuselage as that was just the odd bit of gash Flack and if we got hit we would not see it anyway. Having spent the past year repairing Blenheims and Wellingtons which had been damaged on daylight operations, I believed them.

Six aircraft took part in the operation, taking off at intervals. Our aircraft took off at 19.15 hrs after several false starts, apparently because our intelligence people kept finding out that the Germans had found out our take-off times. Eventually we were ordered suddenly to take off without delay.

As far as I can remember, the other crew members were:-

Captain F/O Warren 2nd Pilot Sgt Greaves* Navigator Sgt Wilson Wireless Operator: Sgt Hogg. I cannot recall the name of 2nd Wireless Operator or Wireless Operator flying as Rear Gunner.

Our flight to the target area was fairly uneventful, although I do remember that we received a wireless signal warning us to keep away from the Portsmouth area as that city was being attacked by a German air raid. (Cf "Friendly Fire")

We had been briefed to attack the target in a succession of runs over the target, dropping a stick of bombs on each run. This had the dual purpose of illuminating the target and give the Navigator a marker for the next run.

As we approached the target area , I checked my instruments and made an entry in the Engineer's log. I then changed over the petrol tanks, so that we would have full tanks while over the target without the danger of running out while we were in action. I then went to a position near the rear entrance where the flares were stowed and the flare chute was situated. I broke out and loaded the beam guns

---

*This was W/O Stan Greaves DFM who was present at our service of Dedication on Sunday, 9th March 1997, at Merrist Wood Agricultural College, Worplesdon, Surrey.

on both port and starboard positions and then proceeded to prime the first flare ready for use and stowed it in the flare chute ready for release. I was fascinated by the lights flashing up all round me. They were of various colours and shapes and some of them appearing to come towards us in a series of dashes, while others seemed to suddenly burst out in sprays like bunches of multi-coloured flowers, at the same time searchlight beams were flashing around trying to pick us up in their beams. I remember thinking that it was the best Firework Display I had ever seen.

Suddenly the Captain's voice came over the inter-com to tell us that the Germans were putting up a 'Box Barrage' and that we had no alternative but to flying straight through it. As we came up on our first run the Navigator's voice intoned over the inter-com, 'Right, right - left, left - right a little - steady - steady - bombs gone.' I dropped my flare and said, "Flare gone," and turned to get the next flare ready. As I turned there was a very bright flash and a large bang from the the front starboard side of the aircraft. My immediate thought was, 'It's only a bit of gash Flack falling on the wing.' The next instant there was a gasp of pain over the inter-com followed by the Captain's voice, 'Who's wounded?' The Navigator's voice replied, "It's me, Wilson, Captain.' 'How serious is it?' 'I've been hit in the knee, but I can carry on with the next run.'

We carried out a further three runs over the target and then started for home.

I secured the beam guns and flare chute, and returned to the Engineer's position behind the pilot and checked my instruments and noted that the starboard inner engine's coolant temperature gauge was going off the clock and that the hydraulic pressure had gone down slightly. I informed the Captain and suggested that we feather the port inner engine, which we did. We continued our flight on three engines.

The Navigator informed the Captain that he was in some pain and needed some assistance to get back to his navigation table. The two

28

wireless operators went to his assistance. At their request, the second Pilot and myself helped them to carry him to the rest position. On examination we discovered that his knee-cap had been shattered. We dressed his wound as best we could and made him as comfortable as possible but he insisted on giving us a course back to base before I gave him an injection of Morphine and painted an 'M' on his forehead.

Sgt Greaves, the second Pilot, noted that the undercarriage light kept flickering and I realized that apart from a damaged engine we also had a hydraulic leak. I was able to correct this with a few occasional strokes on the hydraulic hand pump. I advised the Captain that when the time came to land, he should attempt to lower the flaps and undercarriage in the normal manner, and if he was unsuccessful I would operate the emergency system. (In the event the flaps and undercarriage operated normally.)

The second Pilot was instructed to check our course and navigate us back to base. The second Wireless Operator sat in the nose turret looking for landmarks and Aerodrome Identification Lights.

Just before landing the Captain informed Linton-on-Ouse tower that the aircraft was damaged and requested a Medical Officer and ambulance to be standing by to attend to Sgt Wilson.

The tower acknowledged our message and informed us that there were bomb craters at the beginning of the runway and care should be taken not to undershoot or land short.*

Sgt Wilson was taken to York Military Hospital where he was operated on immediately. I believe his shattered knee-cap was removed and replaced by a silver plate. I paid him a couple of visits in hospital but he did not return to the Squadron before I was shot down and taken prisoner of war on 24 July 1941.

I recall that one of the other aircraft flown by Sqdn Ldr Gilchrist, a Canadian, was shot down in the area of Portsmouth after success-

---

* Whilst the main German attack that night was against Portsmouth, a series of lesser raids were carried out on a number of towns, aerodromes and rural areas in the north.. Linton was one in particular.

fully bombing the target. Apparently he was attacked by an RAF night fighter flown by a Polish pilot engaged on the defence of Portsmouth who wrongly assumed that any bomber aircraft in the vicinity must be the enemy. The Engineer, Sgt Aedy, was very seriously injured and was thrown out of the aircraft by some of the crew while one of them held onto the ripcord. Sqdn Ldr Gilchrist ordered the crew to abandon the aircraft immediately. He baled out of the pilot's escape hatch. He and Aedy were the only survivors. The rest of the crew perished.

Although this was described as a Nursery Raid, one of the crew confided to me later that it was his hairiest operation to date, and he had previously completed a tour on Whitleys."

Sergeant "Oggie" Ogden *(d 1996)*

Merrist Wood
A Brief History

The name 'Merrist' is probably derived from the Old English 'Mere hyrst', being a 'Wood by the pool'. As far back as 1318 a family of 'Merehurst' or 'de Merhurst' lived in Worplesdon, possibly taking their name from the locality.

MERRIST WOOD HALL. – *Front Gable and Chimney, (from a Woodcut 1877).*

(with permission)

The original Merrist Wood Hall was built in 1877 by Mr Norman Shaw, RA. It is a splendid example of the traditional image of his type of house: of moderate size with fine tile hanging and bargate stone, dominated by the half-timbered projecting gable at the West end and the large two-storey window on the side.

At one time there were eleven gardeners, butler, boy, footman, nan

31

-ny, cook, parlourmaid, lady's maid, two housemaids, two chauffeurs, two grooms and a gamekeeper.

Surrey County Council became interested in acquiring Merrist Wood estate in the immediate pre-war years for use as a mental institution, but there was much local opposition to this plan. The war intervened and Merrist Wood became an evacuation centre for the Senior Officers of the County council. After 1945 it was handed over to the Education Department for the establishment of the Surrey Farm Institute.

The first course in Agriculture began in 1948 with 23 students. (40 places had been allocated with a reservation of 20 for ex servicemen.)

The land totalled over 600 acres and needed a lot of attention.

(Minty's field, where L9489 came to rest, was part of this area and had been used for dairy farming by the owner who gave his name to the field. Even today local residents refer to it as such.)

50 acres were set aside for the horticultural department and, apart from outdoor vegetables, a herd of 30 dairy Shorthorn cows and a flock of 50 Clun ewes were introduced. Pigs arrived in 1947 and poultry in 1948.

(It is noted that the first Principal, Mr F W Hankinson, was given an allowance to maintain a horse to travel the estate.)

During the next fifty years the College increased in student numbers and the complexity of the courses on offer. The only major set-back during this period was the outbreak of Foot and Mouth Disease which affected Worplesdon and led to the slaughter of 134 cattle, 218 pigs and 156 sheep. This was in 1958.

The present Principal, John Riddle, has been, from the early days, most supportive of the proposal to locate the crash site of 'F-Freddie' and to establish the permanent memorial to the memory of her crew. It was the College, in conjunction with the Parish Councils of Normandy and Worplesdon, who purchased the engraved plate and constructed the plinth.

32

The Governors have since developed this acreage which now forms the Merrist Wood Golf Club. Our Plaque is close to the fourteenth tee in this beautiful and serene Surrey landscape.

The 'Halifax' 14th Tee: Minty's field 11th November 1997

Peter, Colin, Beryl and Bob   March 1997

Beryl Chandler was a young girl in March 1941 but she remembered visiting the wreckage of 'F-Freddie' and recalled that for many years afterwards engine oil would rise to the surface marking the spot where L9489 had come to earth. (It was she who drew a map to indicate the crash site. This was absolutely accurate, except that a solitary oak tree, used as a marker, had been chopped down during the intervening years.)

Both Bob Wye and his boyhood friend Peter Harms, were able to identify easily the place where they had witnessed the aftermath of the tragic loss of 35 Squadron's first Halifax. They had no hesitation in pointing to the exact location, and this after an absence from the area of 54 years.

Colin Pratley, chairman of the Croydon Aviation Archaeological Society, who had, coincidentally, been interested in this particular aircraft for some time, was now able to verify the actual point of impact by means of an ultra-sensitive metal detector. The readings showed that there was a strong possibility that at least one complete engine was still buried. (The resultant excavation proved this to be so.)

Two weekends of exhaustive digging and sifting revealed the pitiful remains of the forward fuselage and main spar of L9489. The number plate of the Merlin X, when steam-cleaned, confirmed that it was indeed the port inner engine of our aircraft. *(Cf The Merlin X)*

Unearthed Merlin X Engine No 10017

Photograph by N Miller and information by Colin Pratley)

Correspondence with Rolls Royce Aerospace group has revealed that this particular engine was one of a double batch:

        9185- 9191: four off Merlin X

        9193-10183: 496 off Merlin X.

Together these 500 engines comprised Order Number 4770 and Contract Number 829079/38 (the oblique being the year of placement).

All 500 engines were produced at the Rolls Royce Shadow Factory at Crewe, now [in 1996] the home of Rolls Royce Motor Cars Limited:

        9185-9191: tested on 14 July 1940

        9193-10183: tested earlier, between 14 October 1939 and 14 April 1940.

It is interesting to note that all Merlins were odd numbered. Engine number 10017 was built during the week of 3 March 1940 and despatched in the week ending 16 March 1940. Its Air Ministry serial number was A137129 and the record card [AM Form 1180] shows this to be the port inner engine fitted to Halifax L9489.*

Remains of a propeller blade

---

* The starboard outer engine, A137102, and the inner, A137117, caught fire as a result of the night fighter's attack [AM Form 1180]and there was evidence of this from the pieces of casing recovered from the excavation. It is clear that the port outer engine, A137027, was recovered by the crash team shortly after the tragedy. No trace was found.

Part of one propeller blade was discovered close by. Strangely, it is metal, although the first production batch of Halifaxes were fitted with wooden blades.

(cf Aerodata International No 7 p125, et alia.)

(Reproduced by kind permission of the Mansfield "Chad")

During the excavation of the remains of L9489, amongst the fragments that were brought to the surface, the writer's attention was caught by the glint of a small metal object. Upon closer inspection it turned out to be a charred and blackened cigarette lighter.

Obviously, it had belonged to one of the crew in the front section of the Halifax which had impacted in the soft earth and had sunk to more than ten feet under the ground.

Contact with the relations of Pilot Officer Arnold and Sergeants Broadhurst and Lucas revealed that Reg Lucas was the only cigarette smoker. It seemed reasonable to assume that the lighter had belonged to him.

With this in mind, an approach was made to Ronson plc who kindly refurbished the lighter and, through their representative, Linda Bruton, returned the Ronson to the surviving brother and sister of the second pilot.

This was a very emotional occasion for all involved, but the lighter was at last home in Mansfield after an absence of fifty-five years.

The photograph opposite shows, from left to right: Linda Bruton, of Ronson plc; Dennis Hoppe, researcher; Ron Lucas, Reg's brother; his wife Doreen and Nance Burgin, the sister of Sergeant Pilot Reg Lucas, RAFVR.

The Ronson cigarette lighter restored to pristine condition.

Memorial Address

"I would like to present a brief account of the events which have brought us together today and in this most special place. Also, I wish to thank the many people who have been involved over the past two and a half years and have helped and encouraged me in my enquiries.

It was Bill Chorley who, in his book, "RAF Bomber Command Losses: 1941" brought to my attention the fact that a Halifax had crashed nearby, in Normandy, in 1941. It had been returning from the first operation flown by these bombers and had been shot down by a British night fighter. I was intrigued. I now had the time; I wished to know more.

My first visit was made, in October 1994, to the parish church of Normandy (Wyke). There was nothing commemorated in the church, nor were there any service graves in the cemetery.

Elderly people to whom I spoke in the village, and who had been resident in Normandy during the war years, remembered nothing about a plane crash in the area.

The Library in Guildford was my next call and I scrutinised the columns of the Surrey Advertiser for March and April 1941. Nothing was reported due, possibly, to wartime censorship.

A letter to the Surrey Advertiser, the following month, November, brought several positive replies and, at last, I was able to pinpoint the crash site, thanks to the help of Bob Wye, Peter Harms and Beryl Chandler (who kindly drew a map of the location). This was then verified by Colin Pratley, of the Croydon Aviation Archaeological Society, by means of a highly sensitive metal detector. (Colin had also, and coincidentally, been researching this particular Halifax and its fate.)

At this point I determined that no longer should the names of these six young airmen be forgotten in this part of Surrey where four of them had so sadly met their deaths. It would be fitting that a me-

40

morial should be erected for posterity.

Formerly privately owned and known as Minty's Field, the crash site was now situated on property belonging to Merrist Wood Agricultural College. An approach was made to the Principal, John Riddle, who enthusiastically welcomed my plan for a memorial to commemorate this tragedy of war. With the permission of the governors and the help of Tony Begg, Estate Manager, and Steve Townsend the Farm Manager, the Parish Councils of Normandy and Worplesdon and the determined and laborious efforts of the members of the Croydon Aviation Archaeological Society, our Halifax was unearthed. Apart from the complete Merlin engine and other artefacts, a cigarette lighter was discovered. (This was kindly renovated by Ronson plc and I was able to return it some time later to the family of the pilot, Reg Lucas, in Mansfield.)

My next task, in the meantime, was to try and trace the relatives of the six crew members.

Miss Koch, of the War Graves Commission, provided details of the burial places of the four airmen who had died.

The nearest was in Leatherhead: the observer, Teddy Arnold.

Thanks to the kindness of the vicar, David Eaton, I was able to visit a youthful nonagenarian, George Dench, who lovingly reminisced about Teddy Arnold and his family. Through this contact I was able to trace and speak with Mary Millsted, Teddy's surviving sister.

I must thank the local presses for publishing my letters in Folkestone, Coggeshall and Mansfield. Also the parish magazines of Leatherhead and Normandy (Wyke). Without such publicity the relatives of Reg Lucas and Stan Broadhurst would not be present at this ceremony.

I have to thank the 35/635 Squadron Association for putting me in touch with Carol Henderson, the daughter of the captain, the late Air Commodore, Peter Gilchrist.

When I was almost despairing, the Clerk of Coggeshall Parish Council, David Warren, was able to provide the address of Paul

Cooper, the nephew of Bert Cooper, the rear gunner of "F-Freddie".
And, finally, almost at the eleventh hour, the London telephone
directory listed four subscribers with the surname of Aedy. The
second telephone call providentially connected me with Ken Aedy,
Ron Aedy's cousin, living in Ongar, Essex. Through him I was able
to write to Ron's brother, in Canada, and, finally, to his widow,
Audrey, in Australia.

It is reassuring to know that each family of the airmen we commemorate today has been made aware of our project and all, save one,
Carol Henderson, whose home is in Canada, have been able to join
in our act of Dedication.

I cannot let this moment pass without a grateful thank you to all the
veterans of Bomber Command including the standard bearer, Bill
Wallis, and, in particular, one remarkable pilot, Warrant Officer
Stan Greaves. Stan flew on the same operation as "F-Freddie" in
"G-George" and was later shot down and made a prisoner of war.
He was determined, even at great personal sacrifice, to be here this
afternoon. At first, he had planned to fly down from Yorkshire, but
when he realised that this might inconvenience me, he decided to
drive from Pudsey with his 'co-pilot'. (By means of his characteristic
charm, he persuaded RAF Lyneham to detail a single Hercules to fly
past during our ceremony as a tribute to fallen comrades.
Unfortunately, this had to be cancelled at rather short notice due to
"service commitments".)

Before I conclude there are other people I wish to thank: the bugler,
from the Guildford Friary Band, who played the Last Post. The
officials of the Public Records Office, Kew, who showed me around
the complexities of that vast store of resource material. Ernest
Hardy, aviation historian, of Fleet, Hampshire, for imparting his
expertise in the early days of my searches. At RAF Linton-on-Ouse,
I had the good fortune to meet Peter Naylor, who is in charge of the
Memorial Room. His encouragement and service experience proved
invaluable.

42

Without the presence of the chaplain of the college, Roger Robins, and the vicar of Wyke (Normandy), Andrew Knowles, this service of dedication would not have been possible. I thank them both most sincerely. Two and a half years ago I vowed that the names of these airmen should never again be forgotten in this locality. Whilst writing almost 180 letters during this time, I have lived through that fatal night so often and in my thoughts suffered with the crew of "F-Freddie" and their relatives. These young men, the four who died, and the two who survived, typify those who served in Bomber Command during 1939 - 1945: the 55,000 aircrew, all volunteers it must be remembered, who gave their lives, and the thousands who fought for our freedom and lived to tell the tale. We must not forget the debt we owe. For me, my task is now complete, and I feel privileged and honoured that you have been able to join me today in this solemn act of Dedication and gratitude. Thank you".

A family pays its respects. Mary Millsted, sister of P/O Teddy Arnold, with her family and lifelong family friend, George Dench. Sunday 9 March 1997.

The Memorial Plaque

Halifax L9489 of 35 Squadron was shot down by "friendly fire" whilst returning from its first operational sortie on the night of 10 March 1941.
This plaque is dedicated with gratitude to the memory of those who died on this spot:
Sgt R Lucas (Pilot) P/O E Arnold (Observer)   Sgt S Broadhurst (Wireless Operator) F/O A Cooper (Gunner) and to those who survived but have since died:
S/L P Gilchrist (Captain) Sgt R Aedy (Flight Engineer)

"Greater love has no man than this, that a man lay down his life for his friends."
(Jn 15:13)

"Friendly Fire"

This euphemism is now very much part of our language and has been quoted by the media in all recent armed conflicts. It was first used by the Americans during the Gulf War in 1991 to describe incidents when Coalition forces suffered casualties or attacks from their own allies. (This paradoxical term is very misleading: it does not matter who is behind the guns that are pointing at you; the fire is still lethal - far from friendly!)

During the Second World War, when such misfortunes happened all too frequently, especially in the air, people would say almost casually that, *"Oh! he was shot down by one of our own, you know."* These misfortunes were accepted stoically by families, and the nation, as part of the high price paid in the pursuit of peace and justice in a war-torn world.

The crash report card [AM Form 1180] for our Halifax, 'F-Freddie', states in a few precise words, *"Shot down by British fighter."*

As a result, this unexpected tragedy of war brought suffering and misery to four families and anxiety to two other families.

The unfortunate pilot who made such an error of judgement had to live with this memory for the rest of his days. But what of the relatives of those who died and the two airmen who survived? At first there was the incredulity: how could this have happened over England? Surely not a British night fighter; surely not. When the harsh reality of the situation became a brutal fact and no longer a bad dream, it was almost too unbearable to forgive. And yet forgive they did. For some, however, the pangs of resentment took years to heal. Mrs Audrey Aedy, the widow of Sergeant Ron Aedy, the Flight Engineer who was wounded in the attack but survived, revealed that her husband carried the name of the luckless fighter pilot in his wallet for fifteen years after the attack. Such was the inward bitterness he felt. (One can but sympathize: Ron Aedy spent months in hospitals, walked with a limp and never flew operationally again

45

even though his love for flying remained.)

Mary Millsted, the only sister of Pilot Officer Teddy Arnold, the Observer, told how she grieved for the loss of a dear brother who was talented in so many ways. And yet her mother, a woman of great compassion, insisted that her son be laid to rest next to the body of a German airman who had been buried in a remote spot of the cemetery of the parish church, St Mary and St Nicholas, Leatherhead, known as Tramps Corner. Mrs Arnold regularly tended both graves until Unteroffizier Menningmann was reinterred after the war in his homeland.

Sergeant Lucas, the second pilot, was reported as missing at first but then followed news of his death from his injuries the day after the crash. The loss of a gifted son and brother brought numbness and disbelief. When Reg's father travelled to RAF Linton-on-Ouse to collect his son's personal effects, he met Squadron Leader Peter Gilchrist who broke down in tears when he recounted the events of that fateful night. His crew had been exceptional; now four were dead and one seriously wounded. (In later years, before his retirement from the service, Peter Gilchrist met the former fighter pilot who had mistakenly shot down 'F-Freddie', at a reception held in the British Embassy in France. What words passed between them are not recorded.)

The mother of Flying Officer Bert Cooper, the rear gunner and squadron gunnery officer, suffered further distress when, acting upon the instructions of the undertakers, E Finch & Sons Ltd of Aldershot, the coffin remained sealed and she was never to see her son's face again.

What were the circumstances then that led to the loss of 35 Squadron's Halifax L9489 on that ill-fated mission?

Portsmouth was the target for 244 aircraft of Luftflotten 2 and 3 on the night of 10/11 March 1941. This was the largest raid on the mainland since Manchester was bombed on December 22 1940. It was a mixed force of Heinkel 111s and Junkers 88s. The attack

46

lasted from 2000 hours until 0245. (During this time 35 Squadron Halifaxes would have been crossing the channel on the return leg to Linton-on-Ouse.)

Defensive night fighter patrols were flown, as recorded in the Air Controller's record: "*Squadrons active 10/11 March: 264, 610, 616 Selsey Bill/Beachy Head between 2046-2150. Spitfire of 610 at 13,000' saw Heinkel 111 same height. E/A seen to dive into sea. Beaufighter of 219 at 1915 detected E/A near Beachy Head but lost contact. Defiant from Ford 1945 chased 3 E/A between 6-12,000' but haze and cloud.*" [AIR24 534] Three German aircraft were claimed destroyed and one probable. In fact two were lost, both Junkers 88s.

Significantly, Squadron Leader I M Davies, the Air Controller, noted later, that "*friendly bombers flew into Selsey area from the South East and caused uncertainty of identification: very little NIF showed.*" [ibid] The only other targets attacked that night were Cologne and St-Nazaire. Therefore, it seems likely that the poor showing of Night Identification Friendly should be attributed to the small formations of Blenheims and Halifaxes that had raided Le Havre that night.

There was little or no cloud and the visibility was moderate to good, but poor locally inland.

The mobile GCI (Ground Controlled Interception) station that would have alerted a British night fighter to the unidentified intruder was based in a field at Durrington, near Worthing.*

The legendary "Cat's-eye" Cunningham, who was engaged in an un-eventful patrol that night whilst stationed at Middle Wallop with 604 Squadron and 10 Group, recalls that, at this stage of the war, final identification had to be made visually. The Halifax was still on the secret list and although fighter pilots had been made aware that the four-engined Stirling was in service, it had a single tail fin; the

47

Halifax had four engines but two tail fins. Also, in profile, the wedge-shaped twin fins of the early Halifaxes and the general fuselage shape, without the engines being outlined, could have given the appearance of a Heinkel 111. Maybe the British night fighter pilot was not yet aware of this new shape in our skies and thus presumed, tragically, that this was a German bomber. (A Heinkel was claimed as a 'probable' in the Guildford-Horsham area that night; attacked at 18,000 and about the time that 'F-Freddie' was shot down.)

Ironically, two directives were issued by Fighter Command, shortly after L9489 had been destroyed, deploring the fact that some of our own aircraft, mainly bombers, had been shot down by our own fighters due to mistaken identity. In future all Station Commanders were to make certain that their pilots were familiar with the silhouettes and photographs of all aircraft, friend as well as foe. Should similar incidents happen in the future, a Court of Inquiry must be convened.

At the time of the loss of 'F-Freddie', no official inquiry was held and therefore no documentation exists. A number of 35 Squadron veterans still believe that it was an anonymous Polish pilot who destroyed their squadron's Halifax that night, but records show that the two Polish Spitfire squadrons in 11 Group, and 302 at Westhampnett and 303 at Northolt, were not flying on the night of 10 March 1941. Various aircraft have been mentioned: Beaufighter, Blenheim, Defiant, Hurricane and Spitfire. Examples of each were in the air on the night in question.**

In conclusion, perhaps it is fitting that the mystery remains unsolved.

No disclosure now will ever bring back the dead nor alleviate the sufferings that each family has borne during these intervening years.

GCI Station: Durrington, West Sussex. (Code-named "Boffin")
(Pat Burgess & Andy Saunders)

---

* The writer remembers this site well, and often cycled past the unit on his way from school to help the war effort by lifting potatoes at a nearby nursery. (This still exists - in the form of a garden centre, but is no longer dependent upon cheap schoolboy labour!)

* *In the possession of the writer is a piece of the fuselage skin belonging to our Halifax and still bearing the drab, black camouflage paint. It came to light whilst the excavation was taking place, together with other pitiful remains of L9489. Significantly, there is a shell hole in this metal fragment: a piece of 20mm dowelling passes through easily. Only the Beaufighter had 20mm cannons.

49

The Caterpillar Club

Membership of the Caterpillar Club was eagerly sought after by the many thousands of aircrew whose lives were saved by the parachutes manufactured by the Irving Air Chute of Great Britain Ltd.
Peter Gilchrist wrote to the company shortly after his escape from the doomed L9489. He also included Ron Aedy in his application made towards the end of March 1941.
A reply from the Company, dated 9 April 1941 requested further information.

(By courtesy of Irvin Aerospace)

In his consequent correspondence, a fortnight later, Squadron Leader Gilchrist wrote, *"In reply to your letter of April 9th I hereby confirm that the jumps made by Sgt R G Aedy and myself were made with the Irvin type parachute.*
The jumps were made about 22.15* on March 10th between Guildford and Aldershot.
Sgt Aedy was wounded and fainted immediately after leaving the aircraft.
I left the aircraft at approximately 900' and to the best of my knowledge about 4 seconds elapsed between the time when the chute was fully open and when I landed uninjured.
I hope this will enable you to enrol us as members of the Caterpillar Club as Sgt Aedy is still in hospital and has written to me about the matter on two occasions."
To this letter, Irving Air Chute responded, *"We thank you for your letter of the 26th April and we are very pleased to hear that your own*

---

*The time of the crash, it will be recalled, was given as 22.40,on the crash card AM form 1180.

and Sgt Aedy's jumps were made with Irvin parachutes.

We now have much pleasure in welcoming you as members of the Caterpillar Club and will gladly forward your caterpillar pins as soon as they have been engraved with your names, which we hope will be within a week or so.

We are very sorry to hear that Sgt Aedy is still in hospital and trust that he will soon be fully recovered from his injuries."

The two pins were duly despatched on the 12th June with a covering note, *"Further to our letter of 1st may, we have much pleasure in sending your caterpillar pin herewith and trust that you will accept this with our compliments.*

We hope that Sgt Aedy is now quite fit again* and we should be grateful if you would kindly forward his pin with our compliments and best wishes."

SPECIALISING IN SAFETY PARACHUTES

𝕴𝖗𝖛𝖎𝖓𝖌 𝕬𝖎𝖗 𝕮𝖍𝖚𝖙𝖊 𝖔𝖋 𝕲𝖗𝖊𝖆𝖙 𝕭𝖗𝖎𝖙𝖆𝖎𝖓, 𝕷𝖙𝖉.

Directors : L. L. IRVIN (U.S.A.), F.R.Ae.S., F.R.S.A.; Group Capt. SIDNEY SMITH, D.S.O., A.F.C.; EDWARD S. SCEALES

ICKNIELD WAY, LETCHWORTH, HERTS, ENGLAND

Telephone: LETCHWORTH 888 (2 lines)   Cable & Telegraphic Address: "IRVIN, LETCHWORTH"

Company headed notepaper of 1941

---

*Ron Aedy was to spend many more months in hospital convalescing and would never return to operational flying.

Acknowledgements

During the past four years it has been my good fortune to correspond with, and to meet, a large number of people who had one thing in common: each had some connection with the same wartime incident - the loss of Halifax L9489 and four members of its crew at 10.40 on the night of 10 March 1941.

For families and friends of those who died, the recall of this event has brought back painful memories; for those who had shared the terrors of war in Bomber Command, gratitude at having been in the company of such brave men and to have survived the conflict; and for those too young to remember, the desire to perpetuate the memory of those who gave their lives for freedom's sake.

It would not be possible to list everyone who has assisted me in my resolve to establish a permanent memorial in this corner of a Surrey field and therefore those whom I name are representative of those whose names may have been omitted:

Audrey, John & Eileen and Ken Aedy; Mr S Arthur; Mr H Bailey; Martin Barlow; Mrs A Beardsley; Tony Begg; Peter Blakiston; Stanley Blay; Peter Bond; Edward Brett; Mrs M Broadhurst; Mrs Linda Bruton; Nance Burgin; Miss S Carter; Beryl Chandler; Graham Collyer; Ernie Constable; Alan Cooper; Jon Couch; Albert Cunningham; G/C John Cunningham; George Dench; Rev D Eaton; Randy Florence; John Foreman; Mr D Freeman; Frank Gee; Bernard Grady; Stan Greaves; Derrick and Janet Gray; R N Hammond; Ernest Hardy; Peter Harms; Frank Harper; Betty Harris; Mr M L Hatch; Keith Haywood; Carol Henderson; Bill Higgs; Gordon Hogg; Doris Ikin; Sally Jenkinson; Guy Jennings; Rev Andrew Knowles; Miss E Koch; David Lamb; S/L Wally Lashbrook; Claire Lawrence; Mrs M Laws; Ron and Doreen Lucas; Mr and Mrs G Mallatratt; Mrs Marchant; Sam McCauley; Ron McGill; N Miller;

Mrs Mary Millsted; John Mullard; Peter Naylor; Gordon "Oggie" Ogden; Simon Parry; Kenneth Peasgood; Mrs I Phillips; Colin Pratley; Derek Reed; Clive Richards; John Riddle; George Ritchie; Mr D Roberts; Joan Rowland; Mrs Jill Rutter; Andy Saunders; Lorraine Sheldon; Miss J Simpson; John Spelman; Bill Stevenson; Norman Stockton; Mrs B Stone; Mrs J Summerfield; Mrs M Sutcliffe; Mrs C Tester; Dennis Thompson; Steve Townsend; Alan Vial; Stan Ward; David Warren; John Watkins; Mrs H Watts; Mr Wayne-Burre; Mrs Allison Welters and Bob Wye.

Also, the following companies, institutions and publications:

Aldershot News & Mail; Betty's Tea Room, York; Board of Governors, Merrist Wood College; Braintree & Witham Times; Canadian High Commission; "Choice"; London; Coggershall Parish Council; Croydon Aviation Archaeological Society; "Flypast"; Folkestone Herald; Gen-Aircrew Association; Glimlamp; "Intercom"; Irvin Aero-space Ltd; MOD Historical Branch; MOD; National Archives of Canada; News International Reference Library; Normandy Parish Council; Nottingham Herald & Post; Pickerings Bookshop, York; PRC Public Archives, Canada; Public Records Office, Kew; RAF Innsworth; RAF Linton-on-Ouse; RAF Museum; RAFA, Guildford; Rolls Royce plc; Ronson plc; Surrey Advertiser; Teletext Ltd; Worplesdon Parish Council and 35/365 Squadron Association.

Epilogue

"In time of war, men strive and die for the protection of their country and their loved ones and for the ideas in which they believe. No sacrifice is too great and no ordeal too bitter to deter the tide of human effort towards victory. Indeed, in the agony and squalor of war, man reached his true greatness but it is only when peace comes that there exist the conditions in which the ideas for which we fought can be achieved.

I have seen two great wars in my lifetime and after each I have seen the political cadres of almost every country in the world fritter away the opportunities which their warriors have created for them. After each war I have seen the return of pessimism and of distrust and the vitiation of human relations by intrigue, fear, greed and dishonesty. Moral standards in matters great and small have sunk appallingly to impossible levels. In short, man in peace has proven unworthy of the dead of two world wars.

This need not be. We are the same men and women who fought beside those who died. We are made of the same stuff which achieved greatness in time of war. Therefore, in peace, let us think and act as aggressively as we did in war, so that we may achieve freedom, fair play, decency and integrity, internationally, nationally and personally - which the dead of two world wars so nobly earned."

AVM Don Bennett CB CBE DSO

54

Books consulted

Aces High: *Shore* 1994
Action Stations 4: Military Airfields of Yorkshire: *Halfpenny* 1982
Aircraft of the RAF since 1918: *Thetford* 1995
Blitz over Sussex 1941-42: *Burgess & Saunders* 1994
Bombing Colours: *Bowyer* 1973
Checking Up on Your Past : *Wilson* 1994
Forty Years On ...1909-1949: *H P Ltd* 1949
From Hull, Hell and Halifax: *Blanchett* 1990
Halifax and Wellington: *Rapier & Bowyer* 1994
Halifax in Action: *Scutts* 1984
Halifax-Second to None: *Bingham* 1986
Halifax Special: *Robertson* 1990
H P Halifax: *Moyes*   *Aerodata International No7*
Handley Page Aircraft since 1907: *Barnes* 1995
Night Fighter: *Rawnsley & Wright* 1957
RAF Bomber Command and its Aircraft 1941-45:   *Goulding &*
Moyes 1978
Royal Air Force Aircraft L1000-N9999: *Halley* 1993
RAF Bomber Command in Fact, Film & Fiction: *Falconer* 1996
RAF Bomber Command Losses 1941: *Chorley* 1993
RAF Bomber Command Squadron Profiles Number 9: *Ward* 1996
The Bomber Command War Diaries 1939-45:   *Middlebrook &*
Everitt 1996
The Blitz: Then and Now Vol 2: *Ramsey (ed)* 1988
The Halifax File: *Roberts* 1982
The H P Halifax: *Merrick* 1990
The History of Merrist Wood: *Crosby (comp)*   *3rd Edition*
The Squadrons of the RAF & Commonwealth 1918-88: *Halley* 1988
The Whitley Boys: *Donnelly* 1991
Wings over Linton (MkII): *Mason* 1997
1941 The Turning Point Part 1: *Foreman* 1993

Index

A

B

L

M

R

S

66